SILVER

and

SILK

TEXTILES AND JEWELRY OF GUIZHOU, CHINA

SELECTIONS FROM THE COLLECTION OF MINGEI INTERNATIONAL MUSEUM

A MINGEI INTERNATIONAL
EXHIBITION DOCUMENTARY

Sponsored by an Anonymous Grant

ISBN 0-914155-15-6

LIBRARY OF CONGRESS CONTROL NUMBER: 2002106055

PUBLISHED BY MINGEI INTERNATIONAL MUSEUM
BALBOA PARK 1439 EL PRADO SAN DIEGO CA 92101
MAILING ADDRESS PO BOX 553 LA JOLLA CA 92038

Terraced rice paddies have existed in the
Leishan County Valley, Guizhou, for 2000 years.

CONTENTS

SHIDONG MIAO APRON
Shidong, Taijiang County
Silk satin- and chain-stitch embroidery on cotton

FOREWORD

Martha W. Longenecker
Founding President / Director, Mingei International Museum

 One of the unexpected joys of being an art museum director is meeting and coming to know members of one's community who share similar passions. It is particularly uplifting when that passion is for Mingei International's mission — furthering understanding of art of all cultures of the world. Our Museum is blessed with many exceptional individuals who devote their time and resources in fulfilling the vision of Mingei International.

One of these extraordinary people is Phila McDaniel, considered to be the first person to escort a study group from America into the relatively unknown Chinese province of Guizhou. Since that 1984 trip to the place she calls "Land of the Silk Dragon," her passion to learn more has prompted her to return again and again — 27 of her 50 trips to China have been extended study tours to Guizhou.

An art historian, with a Master of Fine Arts degree in Asian art and philosophy, and a teacher and lecturer for many years, Phila is well qualified to perceive similarities and distinctions among the many nationalities of Guizhou's 30,000,000 population. Her love of the people and their culture are expressed in her researching, documenting and collecting the art of the people of Guizhou. Her professional skill in photographing the land and the people heightens her capacity to share the unsurpassed beauty of this Asian culture.

Throughout 18 years of coming to know Guizhou intimately, Phila developed an exemplary collection of over 400 embroidered textiles, silver

SHIDONG MIAO SLEEVE PATCH
For *outou* (bright dress)
Shidong, Taijiang County
Cotton "brown shiny cloth" with silk satin-stitch embroidery
Gift of Phila McDaniel

jewelry and other objects used in daily life from many nationalities through-out the province. Its acquisition in 1999 by Mingei International was made possible by the generous contributions from an anonymous donor and the Hamilton-White Foundation. The collection continues to grow. Like a magnet it attracts important, museum-quality gifts — some from Phila McDaniel, others from Tracey Brown, Mary Beth Jernigan, Drs. James P. and Judith A. Kemp, Peter Nelson, Bea and Tom Roberts and Rob Sidner.

After its premiere presentation at our Museum in San Diego, Mingei International will make the collection available in whole or part for travel to other venues in our nation and world. It, along with other Mingei International traveling collections — including ones from Mexico, Japan, Indonesia, India, and the United States of America, will provide more and more people the opportunity of seeing the finest art of the people from all cultures of the world. This is the vision of Mingei International.

In this fast-paced, high-tech, computerized world in which people are increasingly dependent on electricity and resources beyond their direct control for obtaining clothing, food, shelter and even pure water, it is gratifying to know of a place like Guizhou. Equally inspiring is the continuity of these more-than-2,000-year-old cultures, of people living close to the earth and sky and expressing their innate creativity in timeless works of art that enrich and embellish their lives.

Through these arts a new vista is opened on our marvelous Earth, reinforcing the bridge of understanding of the oneness of the East and the West.

GREEN SHINY CLOTH MIAO FESTIVAL CROWN
Chonganjiang, Tian Tang Village, Huangping County
Cut silver with repoussé technique

SHIDONG MIAO SLEEVE PATCH
Shidong, Taijiang County
For *outou* (bright dress)
Cotton "brown shiny cloth" with silk satin- and chain-stitch embroidery
Showing Mother Butterfly or the Silkworm Dragon emerging from her cocoon

THE LAND OF THE SILK DRAGON

The Collector's Commentary

Phila McDaniel

Curatorial Consultant

There is no other place in the entire world that is quite like Guizhou — a remote, mountainous province in southwest China! Accessible mostly by footpath until the late 1980s and relatively undisturbed by the Cultural Revolution, it is the last of China's provinces to open to the West.

Guizhou has a population of 30,000,000 people of diverse, exotic cultural groups inhabiting autonomous areas. They live in harmony with one another in a natural world of terraced villages and farms lining the river valleys of forest-covered mountain terrain. With fertile, terraced paddy fields these largely self-sufficient cultures have existed for over 2000 years.

This is a place inhabited by at least 17 of China's 56 nationalities. Each has numerous, distinctive clans that continue ancient traditions of elaborate dress and adornment in their daily lives and festivals.

Included in this publication are eight of the 17 nationalities living in Guizhou — Lao Han, Dong, Bouyei, Ge Jia, Shui, Yao, Yi and Miao. The Mao are represented by 21 clans — Shidong, Hei Tou (Black Soil), Black, Folded Silk, Dark Blue, Small Flower, Flower, Short Skirt, Long Skirt Mountain, Pheasant, Magpie, Yunwu, Gaopo, Green Shiny Cloth, Hundred Bird, Long Horn, Metal Weaving, Sidecomb, White Collared, Guping and Xi Jia.

Common to all these nationalities is the art of creating richly-embroidered textiles and elaborate silver jewelry, worn especially by unmarried girls at festivals and other formal occasions. Ancient Chinese documents name dress, food, shelter and land as the most important things in life.

Since intermarriage within a village was long forbidden, it has long been the custom for neighboring villages to hold spring and autumn festivals – over 480 annually. In addition to being gatherings for joyous music, dancing, storytelling, feasting and drinking, the festivals provide an opportunity for young people to meet and choose life partners.

At these festivals the attraction of girls' natural charm and beauty is enhanced by their embroidered jackets, intricately dyed and pleated skirts, layers of silver necklaces and bracelets – and their shining hair topped by silver crowns and ornaments. A Miao or Dong girl's family may add annually to her silver adornment, which is sometimes so heavy that she must be assisted in walking.

Most skirts have many pleats — sometimes over 500. A 100-pleat skirt requires 15 meters of cloth. Young Pheasant Miao women from Leishan County look sedate wearing their long, multi-layered aprons; but from the back one sees bouffant nests of mini-skirts, sometimes four or five under long, colorful tail pieces. A saying in southeastern Guizhou is, "the more skirts, the more beautiful." At the festival known as "Dancing on the Flower Covered Slope" held each spring, Miao girls wear a skirt with as many as 40 layers and weighing as many pounds. Since many of the festivals are held far from home, parents willingly trudge along carrying mounds of the skirts for ten or more miles, so that daughters can don their skirts at the festival. If any woman must move to a new house, she must take her wok and her skirts.

Sometimes dress gives clues as to which girls are unmarried. In Zhijin County, for example, skirts of unmarried Miao girls have a light border, whereas skirts of married women have dark borders. Cap styles, headdresses and hairstyles also indicate marital status. At a glance men may know which women may be courted when couples pair off and disap-

continued page 24

GAOPO MIAO HEAD ORNAMENT AND COMB
Bado Village, 19th Century
Silver and wood
Worn with dangles hanging over face

SHIDONG MIAO SLEEVE PATCH
For *outou* (bright dress)
Shidong, Taijiang County
Cotton "brown shiny cloth" with
silk satin- and chain-stitch embroidery

pear into the bamboo groves to sing love songs to each other, making music with a leaf or playing a *lusheng* flute.

All aspects of festival dress and adornment reveal the origin and history of particular nationalities, clans and subgroups. The distinctive colors, patterns and techniques, as well as symbolic and historic design motifs, distinguish the girls' clans and families, in addition to revealing personal attributes, such as creativity, skill and patience.

So important to Guizhou's culture is this traditional visual language that extraordinary time and effort — four or five years in many cases, are devoted to weaving and embroidering these elaborate garments. A frequent village sight is girls sewing by starlight and early morning sunlight, creating their distinctive embroideries.

The photographs in this publication provide a glimpse of countless variations of creative techniques and designs in textiles and jewelry that have evolved over millennia and continue to flourish in Guizhou.

Because most Guizhou nationalities think of silkworms as miniature dragons and use benevolent dragon designs in their embroidery, one may think of Guizhou as "the Land of the Silk Dragon." Ancient myths and exotic traditions are interwoven in this land where mythology is an integral part of daily life — old legends have been believed and passed on over thousands of years. Guizhou is a mystical place where one might expect to encounter a dragon playing in the Qingshuijiang (Blue Water River) – the site of the Dragon Boat Festival each spring!

There are countless design variations among the ten types of Chinese dragons that appear in Guizhou textiles — Buffalo, Fish, Snake, Silkworm, Centipede, Shrimp, Human Head, Flower, Leaf and Fly. One of the

continued page 26

LONG SKIRT MOUNTAIN MIAO FESTIVAL CROWN
WITH TOP ORNAMENT
Langde Village, Leishan County
Cut silver with repoussé technique
Gift of Drs. James and Judith Kemp

nationalities, the Miao, is known for its curling dragon and two-headed dragon designs.

Richly-colored silk satin-stitch embroideries of the Shidong Miao of Taijiang County often show a man riding a dragon side-saddle, grappling with a dragon and even being swallowed by a dragon — but still visible in a kind of x-ray view. Often featured on central panels of aprons is a stylized dragon surrounded by small figures, faces, insects, birds and other playful animals.

A dragon story depicted in Shidong embroidery — a variation on the ancestors of the Miao story, tells of two *jiyu* birds who for 12 years incubated eggs laid by Mother Butterfly that hatched into 12 brothers who became the progenitors of the first 12 Miao tribes.

A myth that may be the origin of the often-seen snake dragon design, depicted on a Shidong sleeve patch, tells of a shaman who told a man that if he was buried in a certain place, he would become a dragon. After he died and was buried, his children — so eager to see whether he had turned into a dragon, dug up the body soon after the funeral. They were amazed to see that his head had, indeed, turned into a dragon; but his body was a snake form, an intermediate state of change.

The Dong people also use many forms of the dragon in their architecture and festival clothing. The Yao believe that they are descendants of Panhu, the ancestor of the "Dragon Dogs" (*Gaoxinshi*). Sometimes a long tail representing the tail of a dragon is pinned to their turbans.

Besides their application in embroidery and weaving, the dragon design is also featured in silver crowns, hairpins and other ornaments. Boats used in the Miao Dragon Boat Festival are decorated with large dragon figureheads carved of willow wood.

The people of Guizhou often give human attributes and qualities to animals they embroider into textiles. The elephant — an emblem of great determination, is sometimes seen as a pillar supporting a house. The dog, monkey, cat and mouse are all depicted as clever and agile while

LAO HAN CHILD'S WAISTCOAT

c. 1850

Silk with embroidery

Three noble Mandarin figures wearing symbols of Long Life, Protection and Prosperity

LAO HAN CHILD'S *TOU-TOU* (BIB)

19th Century

Silk embroidery

LAO HAN BABY COLLAR

19th Century

Silk and cotton

MIAO NECKLACE
Collected from the Long Skirt Miao
Shidong Village, Leishan County
Silver
Gift of Drs. James and Judith Kemp

SHIDONG MIAO WEDDING JACKET
Shidong, Taijiang County, more than 100 years old
Cotton "brown shiny cloth" with silk satin-stitch embroidery
Gift of Tracey Brown

SHIDONG MIAO COLLAR PATCH
For *outou* (bright dress)
Shidong, Taijiang County
Cotton "brown shiny cloth" with applied folded silk and embroidered patch

opposite & page 46   Shidong Miao girls wearing *outou* (bright dress)
and silver ornaments for the Sisters' Colorful Rice Festival

page 47   SHIDONG MIAO JACKET SLEEVE *detail*
For *outou* (bright dress)
Shidong, Taijiang County
Velvet with silk satin- and chain-stitch embroidery
Warriors riding the Fish Dragon and the Buffalo Dragon

pages 49-53   SHIDONG MIAO SLEEVE / SHOULDER PATCHES
For *outou* (bright dress)
Shidong, Taijiang County
Cotton "brown shiny cloth" with silk satin- and chain-stitch embroidery

pages 50-51   Showing mothers and babies *detail*

pages 52-53 Showing a couple wishing for a baby. Unborn souls appear in
a pomegranate shape in the heavens above.

page 54   SHIDONG MIAO BRACELET
Shidong, Taijiang County
Silver

page 55   SHIDONG MIAO CROWN ORNAMENT
Shidong, Taijiang County
Silver

page 56   Shidong Miao woman wearing silver headdress

page 57   SHIDONG MIAO SHOULDER PATCH
For *outou* (bright dress)
Shidong, Taijiang County
Cotton "brown shiny cloth" with silk satin-stitch embroidery. Horsehair wrapped
with silk threads creates raised coils.
Gift of Peter Nelson

pages 58-59   DETAIL OF PAGE 57

opposite   SHIDONG MIAO SLEEVE PATCH
For *oushe* (dark dress)
Shidong, Taijiang County
Cotton "brown shiny cloth" with variegated silk satin- and chain-stitch

Near Guiyang, a Hei Tou (Black Soil) Miao girl is dressed in a
miniature version of an adult costume.

opposite   A Black Miao woman wearing a typical headdress.

FOLDED SILK MIAO NECKLACE
Wenxiang Village, Kaili County
Silver

A small group of Miao in Wenxiang near Kaili are dubbed Folded Silk Miao because they take minute squares of silk and fold them into overlapping triangles to form designs such as dragons, fish or birds which are then sewn onto a colorful background. The strips are held between tiny bamboo sticks while the patches are sewn into jacket sleeves, fronts and collars. Another of their rare techniques is known as *dazi* or *geyi* (piled up) in which single horsehairs are wrapped with silk thread and used as outlines for areas of satin-stitch.

FOLDED SILK MIAO BABY CARRIER WITH DETAIL

Wenxiang Village, Kaili County

Woven cotton and silk with folded silk quilting and *dazi* technique

Gift of Drs. James and Judith Kemp

SMALL FLOWER MIAO JACKET
Luobo River Style, near Guiding
Cotton with patchwork of various embroidery stitches
This rare jacket has a batik pattern panel enriched with embroidery.

FLOWER MIAO APRON *detail*

Anqing Style, Anshun

Cotton with appliqué and embroidery

Small Flower Miao girls play *lusheng* flutes at the Dancing Hillside Flower Miao Festival at Nankai in Northwest Guizhou. Girls make and present collars to boys they wish to marry. A boy will keep only the collar made by the girl of his choice.

SMALL FLOWER MIAO COLLAR
Nankai area, Shuicheng County
Cotton with appliquéd strips and cross-stitch
Gift of Phila McDaniel

SMALL FLOWER MIAO COLLAR
Nankai area, Shuicheng County
Wool with cotton appliquéd strips and cross-stitch
Gift of Phila McDaniel

SMALL FLOWER MIAO COLLAR
Nankai area, Shuicheng County
Cotton with appliquéd strips and cross-stitch

previous pages In the collars of the Small Flower Miao of Nankai village one may see yellow appliquéd strips symbolizing the Yellow River (Huanghe) where their ancestors once lived. Other strips in red represent the Yangtze River valleys and tributaries where this Miao group finally settled. In the cross-stitched and double appliquéd collars, geometric symbols in the middle of concentric lines represent villages in the middle of the fields. The elders of the various villages love to explain the symbolism found in their costumes.

opposite   SMALL FLOWER MIAO REVERSE SIDE OF COLLAR   *detail*
Nankai area, Shuicheng County
Cotton with appliquéd strips and cross-stitch
Gift of Phila McDaniel

page 84   SMALL FLOWER MIAO SHOULDER BAND
Part of "banner dress"
Huaxi, Guiyang County, c. 1920s
Cotton with cross-stitch embroidery
Snowflake pattern showing pig's foot motif

page 85   SMALL FLOWER MIAO PANEL
Part of "banner dress"
Huaxi, Guiyang County
Cotton with cross-stitch embroidery

A centuries' old legend tells of the "banner dress" of the Huaxi Miao, a small group dwelling in the Huaxi area near Kaili. This dress has many parts and gives an example of the finest cross-stitch in Guizhou and perhaps the world. Most Huaxi motifs are based on a pig's foot to form a snowflake pattern.

SMALL FLOWER MIAO PANEL
Part of "banner dress"
Huaxi, Guiyang County, c. 1920s
Cotton with cross-stitch embroidery

SMALL FLOWER MIAO PANEL
Part of "banner dress"
Huaxi, Guiyang County, c. 1920s
Cotton with cross-stitch embroidery

SMALL FLOWER MIAO PANEL
Part of "banner dress"
Huaxi, Guiyang County, c. 1900
Cotton with cross-stitch embro dery showing buffalo horn mo

page 94   SHORT SKIRT RIVERSIDE MIAO BABY CARRIER
Qinman Village, Kaili
Woven silk

page 95   SHORT SKIRT RIVERSIDE MIAO APRON
Qinman Village, Kaili
Silk with appliquéd silk felt

A Pheasant Miao woman greets visitors in Dafang Village, Leishan
County. In her silver crown and silver-studded tunic, she embodies
the Miao idea that girls should be as beautiful as pheasants.

page 100 YUNWU MIAO DETAIL OF *BEI PAI* (COLLAR)
Yunwu Village, Guiding County
Cotton with cross-stitch embroidery and cowry shells

page 101 MAGPIE (YA CHUO OR XI QUE) MIAO COLLAR
WITH *BEI PAI* (NECKPIECE)
Huishui County
Cross-stitch embroidery with cowry shells and silver
The *bei pai* is given as an engagement present
Gift of Phila McDaniel

pages 102-103 GAOPO MIAO BACK PLATE FOR *BEI PAI* (COLLAR)
Bado Village
Woven cotton with embroidery

page 106   GREEN SHINY C_OTH MIAO PANEL   *detail*
Chonganjiang, Tian Tang Village, Huangping County
Dyed cotton with silk satin-stitch embroidery

page 107   GREEN SHINY CLOTH MIAO SMALL BOY'S TUNIC
Chonganjiang, Tian Tang Village, Huangping County
Dyed cotton with silk satin-stitch embroidery
Gift of Phila McDaniel

A Green Shiny Cloth Miao boy wears his festival silver ornaments
and holds a sugar cane piece for a sweet treat.

opposite   GREEN SHINY CLOTH MIAO BABY CARRIER
Chonganjiang, Tian Tang Village, Huangping County
Silk satin-stitch, running-stitch and twisted-thread embroidery

pages 112-113   Green Shiny Cloth Miao skirt showing silk
embroidery, weaving and pleating

Green Shiny Cloth Miao woman at Tian Tang Village is in festival dress with pleated round hat. The hat is the first item girls make around age seven, as training for sewing a wedding costume.

The Green Shiny Cloth Miao women of Tian Tang Village are known for their miniature stitching on skirt hems, baby carriers, caps and jackets. Completion of a costume may take nine years.

opposite   Older women of Langde Village enjoy embroidering and
visiting in the morning sunshine. Continuing traditions, grandmothers
teach their granddaughters old-style techniques.

page 120   A Long Skirt Mountain Miao woman in festival dress offers
visitors rice wine in a buffalo horn. She stands at the entrance gate
to Landge Village in Leishan County, near Kaili City.

page 121 LONG SKIRT MOUNTAIN MIAO HORNED FESTIVAL HEADPIECE
Langde Village, Leishan County
Cut silver with repoussé technique
Gift of Bea and Tom Roberts

Langde Village girls and shaman in processional dance during the
Guzang Fertility Festival — held every thirteen years to ensure
prosperity

page 124   A young resident of Langde Village greets visitors with a
cup of rice wine. All villagers cooperate in offering hospitality.

page 125   LONG SKIRT MOUNTAIN MIAO FESTIVAL CROWN
Langde Village, Leishan County
Cut silver with repoussé technique
Lotus centerpiece with women warriors on horses

opposite   LONG SKIRT MOUNTAIN MIAO FESTIVAL CROWN
WITH TOP ORNAMENT
Langde Village, Leishan County
Cut silver with repoussé technique
Gift of Drs. James and Judith Kemp

pages 128-129 MIAO MAN'S FESTIVAL JACKET
Moon Mountain area, Zaibiang and Xiang Villages, Liping County
Cotton with embroidery and appliqué
Gift of Drs. James and Judith Kemp

opposite   HUNDRED BIRD MIAO FESTIVAL COSTUME
WITH FLYING SKIRT
Congjiang County
Silk felt with cotton appliqué, feathers, Job's-tears seeds and gauze lining
A style now worn by both men and women, but originally worn by male reed
flute players
Gift of Drs. James and Judith Kemp

130

opposite HUNDRED BIRD MIAO FESTIVAL COSTUME
Moon Mountain area, Pinyong, Rongjiang County
Silk felt with cotton appliqué, feathers, Job's-tears seeds and gauze lining
Gift of Drs. James and Judith Kemp

page 134-135   A group of Hundred Bird (Bianaio) Miao at a high mountain village near Sandu greets visitors. They wear impressive woven and embroidered wool and feathered costumes and elegant silver.

Along the Xijiang River one may see a type of overskirt consisting of individual panels of silk, decorated with rich embroidery and colorful tassels. This type of skirt is known as a flying skirt or screen skirt and can be dated to the Qing dynasty (1644-1911). A Miao group living in Langde village in Leishan County near Kaili, called Long Skirt Mountain Miao, wear a flying skirt of this type at festivals. In the area of Congjiang, Ronjiang, Danzhai and Sandu, this type of gala overskirt is often seen with chicken feathers at the bottom of each panel. The Miao groups here are known as Hundred Bird Miao and have several splinter groups that favor certain colors or patterns as backgrounds. Some Hundred Bird Miao have a centipede within a square or diamond shape on the back of the jacket, while other types may feature a dragon or other creature.

pages 136-137   LONG HORN MIAO MAN'S APRON
Suoga Village, Liuzhi area
Cotton with cross-stitch and Job's-tears seeds

pages 138-139   Long Horn Miao girls at Suoga Village wear huge
hanks of ancestral hair, he d in place with wide white bands.

page 140   Metal Weaving Miao weave minute slivers of metal under
embroidered designs. The metal is then visible only on the top side,
and the reverse shows only embroidery.

page 141   METAL WEAVING MIAO APRON
Raohao Village, Jianhe County
Cotton with silk embroidery and metal
Gift of Phila McDaniel

opposite   Metal Weaving Miao near Jianhe greet their first foreign
visitors with rice wine.

opposite   SIDECOMB MIAO BABY CARRIER *detail*
Zhuchang town and Zhijin, Dafang, Qianxi and Nayhang Counties
Cotton with embroidery
This type of embroidery is done on top of fine-lined batik that is invisible when
the embroidery is completed.
Gift of Phila McDaniel

SIDECOMB MIAO JACKET *detail*
Zhijin, Dafeng, Nayong, Qianxi, Qingzhen, Pingba, Puding, Zhenning, Anlong,
Qinglong, and Guanling Counties
Cotton with silk satin- and overcast-stitch embroidery

opposite   WHITE COLLARED MIAO HEADDRESS
Dandu Style in Duyun, Danzhai and Sandu areas
Silver with repoussé technique, feathers and yarn

pages 158-159   GUPING MIAO FESTIVAL JACKET WITH BACK BIB
Conjiang County
"Brown shiny cloth" with cotton embroidery, Job's-tears seeds and feathers

pages 160-161 MIAO BAEY CARRIER
Huangping County
Cotton with silk embroidery, a contemporary adaptation of an old style
Gift of Phila McDaniel

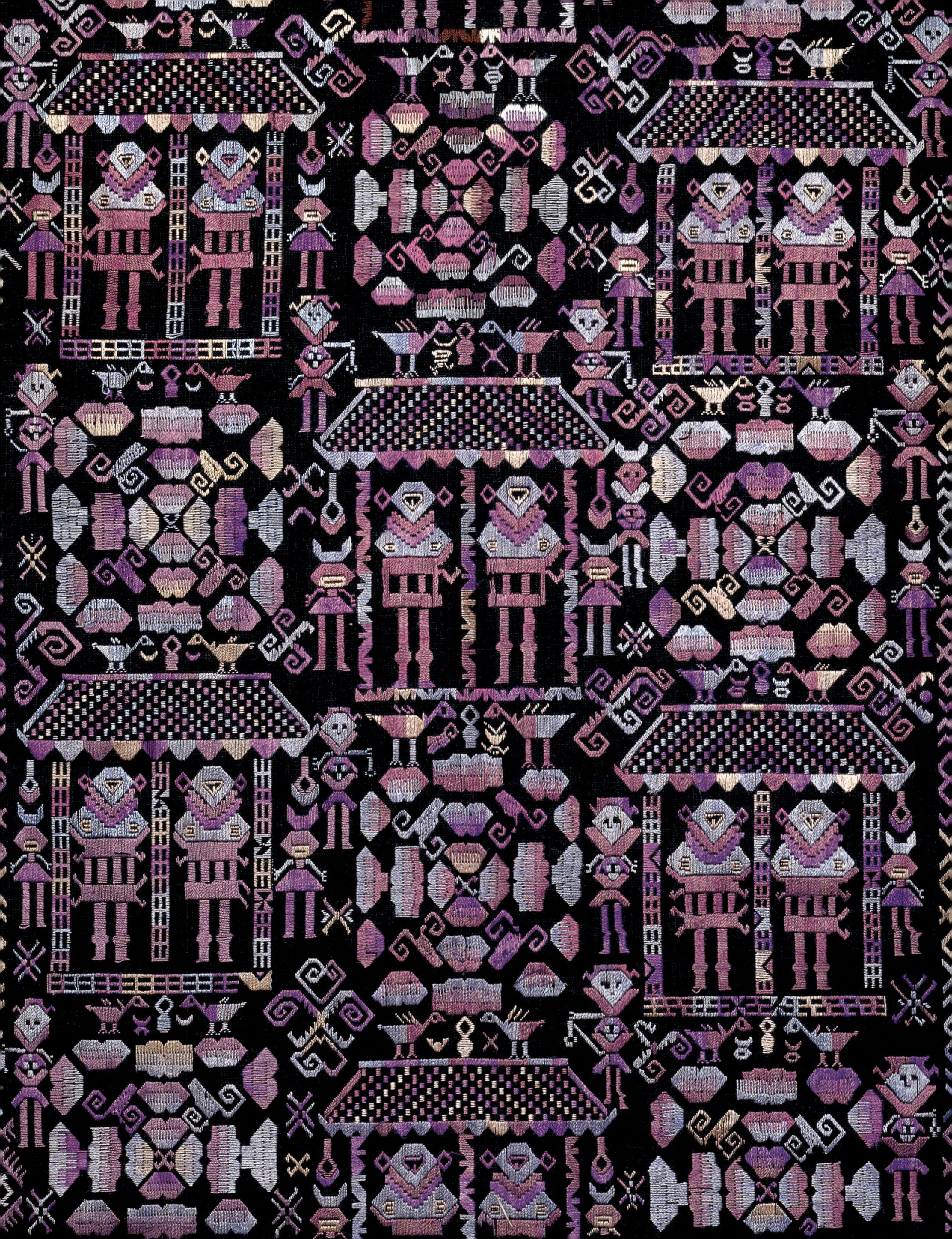

Xi Jia girl wears traditional costume. The Xi Jia are a unique minority group
not yet recognized with special status by the central government of China.

previous pages   Xi Jia batik skirt – pleated, embroidered and appliquéd

opposite   XI JIA HEADSCARF   *detail*
Guiyang area
Cotton and silk embroidery

DONG APRON WEIGHT
Zhaoxing Village, Liping County
Silver
Gift of Drs. James and Judith Kemp

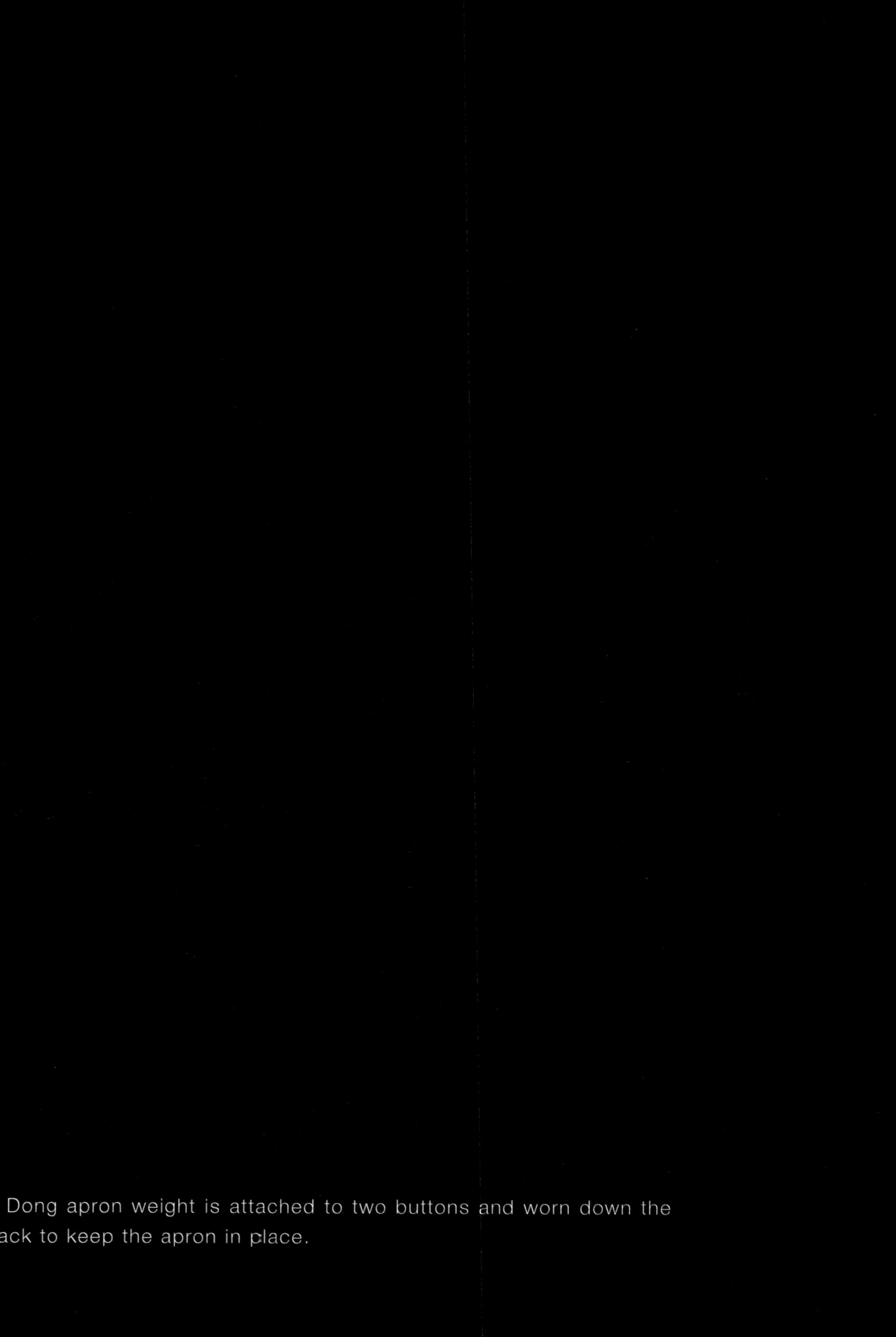

A Dong apron weight is attached to two buttons and worn down the
back to keep the apron in place.

opposite   DONG APRON *detail*
Zhaoxing Village, Liping County, Pre-Cultural Revolution
Embroidery
This pattern and color are traditional for weddings.
Gift of Phila McDaniel

page 174   DONG APRON WITH ANCIENT MOTIFS
Zhaoxing area, Liping County, Pre-Cultural Revolution
Cotton with embroidery
Gift of Phila McDaniel

page 175   DONG PANEL *detail*
Zhaoxing area, Liping County
Brocade
Gift of Phila McDaniel

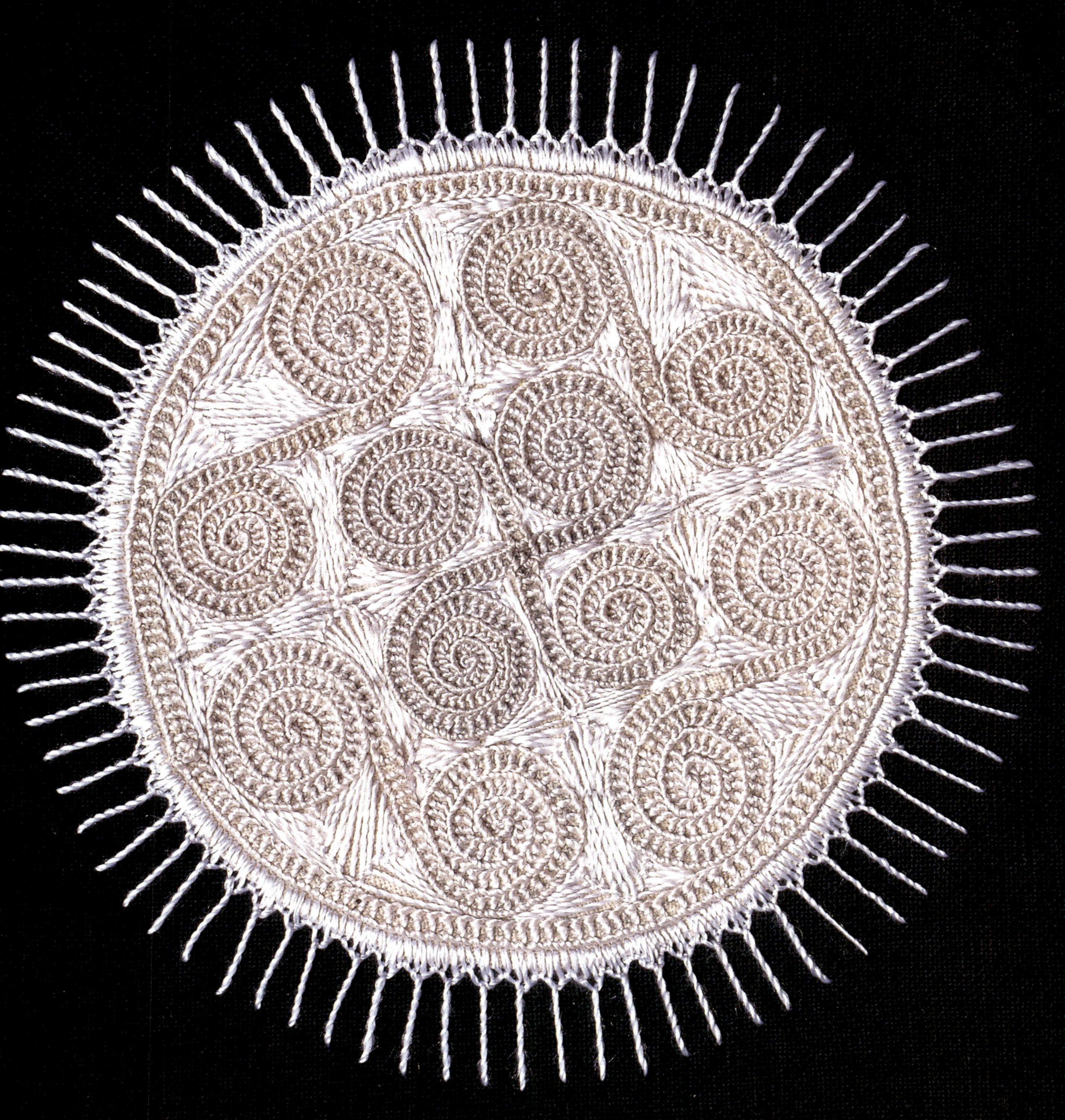

opposite   DONG FESTIVAL TIARA
Zhaoxing area
Silver and cotton
Gift of Phila McDaniel

pages 178-179   During festivals Dong women wear silver headdresses
made of cut silver and feathers. Visitors are escorted three times
through drum tower pillars The women then gather to sing long ballads
in harmonious tones.

Dong people have been famous since the seventh century for making
a textile known as "brown shiny cloth" and using it for many parts of
their clothing, including short knife-pleated skirts for young girls and
complete costumes for men. Some Miao groups make this same type
of cloth in southeast Gu zhou, not far from the Dong areas. It is not
clear which group originated this unusual type of textile technique.

opposite   DONG FESTIVAL GOWN WITH VEST
Zhaoxing area, Liping County
Cotton shiny cloth with embroidery
Gift of Drs. James and Judith Kemp

pages 182-183   SHUI JACKET
Sandu area
Cotton with embroidery and appliqué

opposite   SHUI FABRIC   *detail*
Sandu area
Woven cotton

pages 186-187   GE JIA SLEEVE PANEL
Matang Village, Kaili
Batik with embroidery

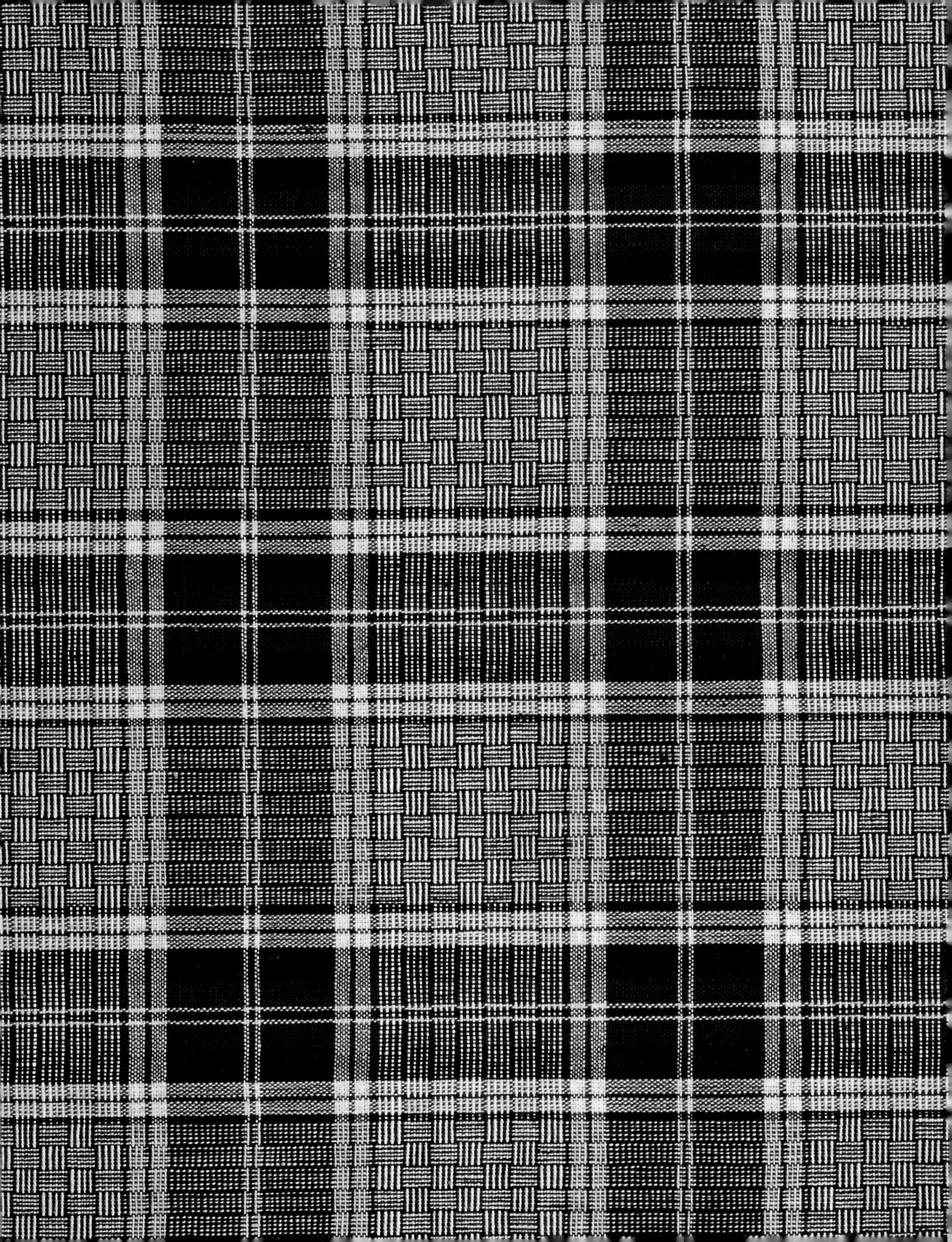

GE JIA BABY CARRIER   *detail*
Matang Village, Kaili, c. 185C
Cotton with silk embroidery and indigo dye

A Ge Jia girl begins at age seven to create the clothing for her future
wedding by making an intricately pleated hat, the design of which has
a long history and military symbolism. Her entire dress, incorporating
batik, weaving and embroidery, is prepared to be finished by the time
she is ready to marry.

opposite   Ge Jia girls in Matang Village, Kaili County are trained to
make long strips for leggings and belts.

pages 192-193   GE JIA BABY TUNIC
Matang Village, Kaili, Pre-Cultural Revolution
Hemp with indigo-dyed batik

page 196   A Bouyei bride on her wedding day at the groom's house
near Sandu. This young bride proves her proficiency in household tasks
by making shoes and innersoles for each new relative, weaving a bag
for each wedding guest ard cooking the Guizhou Hot Pot for guests
and villagers.

page 197   BOUYEI STRIP FOR APRON   detail
Shitou Village, Huangguoshu Falls
Cotton with silk satin-stitch embroidery

BIBLIOGRAPHY

Abadie, Maurice, "Les Races du Haut-Tonkin," *Revue d'Ethnographie et des Traditions Populares,* No. 3, 1922, pp. 81-110.

Adams, Moni, "Dress and Design in Highland Southeast Asia: The Hmong (Miao) and the Yao," *Textile Museum Journal*, Vol. 4. No. 1, 1974.

Anstey, Helen and Terry Weston, *The Anstey Weston Guide to Textile Terms*, London: Weston Publishing Limited,1997. ISBN 0-9530130-0-6.

Bai Xinmin, ed., *The Local Customs and Traditions of the Tujia*, Sichuan National Press, October 1993.

Baker, M., *A Steep Learning Curve: Teaching Techniques from Southwest China, The World of Embroidery,* Vol. 50, No. 4, July 1999, pp. 272-3.

Baker, Muriel and Margaret Lunt, *Blue and White: The Cotton Embroideries of Rural China*, New York: Charles Scribner's & Sons, 1977.

Balfour, Paul J., *Indigo*, London: British Museum Press, 1998.

Bartlett, Magnus, ed., *China Guides, China Unknown*, Hong Kong: China Guides Series Limited, 1985. ISBN 962-217-017-10.

Beijing Arts and Crafts Publishing House, *Costumes and Adornments of Chinese Yi Nationality Picture Album*, Beijing: 1990. ISBN 7-80526-033-8/G.14.

Beijing Dongfang Mingzhu Cultural Development Company, *China's Minority Peoples*, Beijing: China Pictorial Publishing House, 1995. ISBN 7-80024-046-O/J-047.

Berliner, Nancy Zeng, *Chinese Folk Art*, Boston: Little, Brown and Company, 1986.

Bhikkhu, Dhamarasao, and Bhikkhu, Virojano, *The Historical Background and Tradition of the Meo*. Bangkok: The Doi Pui Hermitage, 1973.

Boudot, E., "Minority Costumes and Textiles of Southwestern China," *Orientations*, Vol. 25, No. 2, Feb. 1994, pp. 59-66.

Campbell, Margaret, Nakorn Pongnoi and Voraphitak Chusack, *From Hands of the Hills*, Hong Kong: Media Transasia, 1978.

Carter, Herbert R., *The Spinning and Twisting of Long Vegetable Fibres (Flax, Hemp, Jute, Tow & Ramie)*, Philadelphia: Charles Griffin & Co., Ltd., 1904, 8 vol.

Cen Xiaowen, *The Miao*, National Press, Dec. 1990.

Chaturabhawd, Preecha, *People of the Hills,* Bangkok: Editions Duang Kamo, 1980.

Catlin, Amy, *Music of the Hmong: Singing Voices and Talking Reeds*, Providence RI: Museum of Natural History, Center for Hmong Lore, 1985.

Catlin, Amy, Joanne Cubbs, and Timothy Dunnigan, *Hmong Art Tradition and Change,* Sheboygan: John Michael Kohler Arts Center, 1986.

Central Academy of Ethnology and the People's Art Publishing Company, *Costumes of the Minority People of China,* Kyoto: Goichi Kakimoto, 1982. Code number 075-722-0118.

Chai Fei, Hsu Chen-peng, Cheng Shang-Jen and Wu Shu Sheng, *Indigo Prints of China*, Peking: 1957.

Chan, Anthony, *Hmong Textile Designs*, 1990.

Chen, Guoan, *The Shui*, National Press, 1985.

Chen, Ninkang and Fu Mulan, *Batik Art, Guizhou, People's Republic of China,* Guizhou Educational Publishing House and Guizhou Batik Art Institute, 1986. ISBN 7-80583-410-S/G .409.

Chen, Wen-si, *The History of Chinese Textile Technology, Zhongguuo Fangi Shi*, Beijing: The Science Press, 1984.

Chen, Zhijun, "History Books That Can Be Worn," *China Southern Airlines Gateway Magazine*, March 2001.

Cheng, Te-K'un and Liang Ch'an, *The Southwestern Barbarians, Chengdu, Sichuan, West China Union University Museum Translation Series,* no. 1, 1945.

Cheng, Weiji, Chief Compiler, *History of Textile Technology of Ancient China*, New York: The Science Press, 1992.

Chiang, Pi Jing and Fong, Siu Nang, *Miao Costumes of Southeast Guizhou - Illustrated Research Directory*, Taipei: Textiles and Clothing Graduate Institute of Fu Jen Catholic University, 2000. ISBN 957-9000-92-1.

China Central Minorities Institute, Minzu (Folk Arts Department), *Shidong Embroidery, Jiansu Province,* Embroidery Research Institute, 1995.

China House Gallery, China Institute In America, *Richly Woven Traditions — Costumes of the Miao of Southwest China and Beyond*, New York: China Institute of America, 1987. Library of Congress Catalog Card No. 87-72174.

"China Reconstructs," *China's Minority Nationalities*, Beijing: Great Wall Books, 1984.

Christensen, L. Clair, Mary H. Fong, Pat Hickman, and Joan Randall, *Art of the Hmong Americans*, University of California at Davis, 1985.

Clarke, Robert C and Wengfeng Gu, "Survey of Hemp (*Cannabis Sativa L.*) Use by the Hmong (Miao) of the China/Vietnam Border Region," *Journal of the International Hemp Association*.

Clarke, Samuel R., *Among the Tribes in Southwest China*, London: China Inland Mission, Morgan & Scott, 1911.

Cooper, Robert, et al *The Hmong,* Bangkok: Art Asia Press Co. Ltd., 1991.

Corrigan, Gina, "Geographer Turns Textile Enthusiast in China," *Embroidery,* Vol. 45, No. 2, summer 1994, pp. 98-9.

___________, *Odyssey Illustrated Guide to Guizhou,* Hong Kong: The Guidebook Company, 1985. ISBN 962-21.

___________, "Guizhou Province, Southwest China: Bast Fibers used by the Miao and the Processes Involved," *Newsletter of the Textile Society of Hong Kong,* Vol. 4, No. 3, May 1996, pp. 3-5.

___________, "Hemp and Ramie in Southwest China," *Hali,* No. 113, Nov/Dec. 2000, pp. 81-83.

___________, *Miao Textiles from China,* The Trustees of the British Museum, 2001. ISBN 0-295-98137-7.

___________, "Search and Research: The Pleated Skirts of the Miao," *The World of Embroidery,* Vol. 49, No. 1, Jan. 1998.

de Beauclair, Inez, *Ethnographic Studies: The Collected Papers of Inez de Beauclair,* Taipei: Southern Materials Center, Inc., 1986.

___________, *Tracht und Ornamentik der Pa Miao im Anshun-Kreis der Provinz Kweichow, Studia Serica* (Journal of the Cultural Research Institute) 2, Chengdu, Sichuan, PRC, 1941.

___________, "Tribal Cultures of Southwest China," Vol. 2 of *Asian Folklore and Social Life Monographs,* Taipei: The Orient Cultural Service, 1970.

Ding, Jiarong, *Dictionary of China's Ethnic Folklore,* Hubei Province, PRC: College for Ethnic Communities.

Editorial Committee of "Ethnic Costumes and Clothing Decorations from China" of Shanghai Theatrical College, *Ethnic Costumes and Clothing Decorations from China,* Chengdu, Sichuan, PRC: 1989. ISBN 962 238 145 6 HF-123-3.

Editorial and Writing Task Force for Chinese Ethnic Minorities , *Chinese Ethnic Minorities,* Beijing: National Press, 1981.

Embree, John F. and , Lilian Ota Dotson, *Bibliography of the Peoples and Cultures of Mainland Southeast Asia,* New York: Russel and Russel.

Foreign Affairs Office of Guizhou Provincial People's Government, "Guizhou National Festivals," Guiyang, Guizhou: Guizhou Arts Publishing House, 1957. ISBN 7-5413-0008

Foreign Languages Press, Beijing, A Happy People — the Miaos, Beijing: Foreign Languages Press, 1998. ISBN 7-119-00521-9.

Gao, Hanyu, *Chinese Textile Designs,* London: 1992. ISBN 0670818976.

Garrett, Valery M., *Traditional Chinese Clothing in Hong Kong and South China, 1840-1980,* Hong Kong: Oxford University Press, 1987.

___________, *Chinese Clothing: an Illustrated Guide,* Hong Kong: Oxford University Press, 1994.

___________, *A Collector's Guide to Chinese Dress Accessories,* Singapore: Times Editions Pte Ltd., 1997.

Geddes, William Robert, *Migrants of the Mountains, The Cultural Ecology of the Blue Miao (Hmong Njua) of Thailand,* Oxford: Clarendon Press, 1976.

Geijer, Agnes, *A History of Textile Art,* London: Pasold Research Fund Ltd., in association with Sotheby Parke Bernet Publications, 1979. ISBN 0-85667-055-3.

Gillow, J and B. Sentance, *World Textiles: A Visual Guide to Traditional Techniques,* London: Thames & Hudson, 1999.

Gosta Sandberg, *Indigo Textiles: Technique and History,* London: A &C Black, 1989.

Graham, David Crockett, *Folk Religion in Southwest China,* Washington D.C.: Smithsonian Institute, 1961.

___________, "Songs and Stories of the Ch'uan Miao," *Smithsonian Miscellaneous Collections,* Vol. 123, No.1, Washington D.C.: Smithsonian Institution, 1954.

___________, "The Customs of the Ch'uan Miao," *Journal of the West China Border Research Society,* No. 9, Chengdu, Sichuan: China, 1937.

Grist, Reverend W.A., *Samuel Pollard, Pioneer Missionary in China,* Taipei: Ch'eng Wen Publishing Co., 1971.

Gu, Puyang, Chao Lin Pan, Bai Bo, and Guo Cheng, eds., *China's Nuoxi (Exorcism) Opera (Drama) Survey Report (Diaccha Boegao),* Guiyang: Guizhou People's Publishing House. ISBN 7-221-02516-9/G .1 428.

Guizhou Advertising Company, *Guizhou — A Treasure to be Explored,* (booklet), Guiyang.

Guizhou Cultural Bureau, People's Republic of China, San Francisco Craft and Folk Art Museum, the Asian Cultural Council, New York City and the U.S. China Folk Art Foundation, *Precious Place — Minority Costume and Textiles of Guizhou, China,* San Francisco Craft and Folk Art Museum.

Guizhou People's Publishing House, *Miao Zhuang,* Guiyang, Guizhou: 1992. Text in Mandarin.

Guizhou Provincial Editorial Task Force, *A Social and Historical Survey of the Dong,* Guizhou National Press, 1988.

Guizhou Provincial Museum, *Miaozu Yinshi (Silver Ornaments of the Miao Nationality),* Beijing: 2000.

Guizhou Provincial Tourism Administration and Hong Kong China Tourism Press, *Focus on Guizhou,* 1999. ISBN-962-7799-86-6.

Haks, Leo, *Celestial Art: Paper Offerings and Textiles from China*, Ghent: privately printed, 1997.

Harrell, Stevan, ed., "Cultural Encounters of China's Ethnic Frontiers," Seattle: University of Washington Press, 1995, pp. 92-116, 217-247.

Hong Kong Museum of History, *Ethnic Costumes of the Miao People in China*, 1985. ISBN 962-7033-11-10.

______________, *Archaeological Discoveries of Ancient Yue People in South China*, Hong Kong: Friendship Printing Co. Ltd., 1993.

Honolulu Academy of Arts, *Family Ties in Asian Textiles: Children's and Adult Costumes of China and Japan,* Honolulu: Honolulu Academy of Arts, 2000. ISBN 0-937426-43-1.

Hosie, Alexander, *Three Years in Western China: A Narrative of Three Journeys — Ssu-Ch'uan, Kuei-Chow, and Yun-Nan*, Taipei: Ch'eng Wen Publishing, 1972.

Hua, He, "The Bouyei Funeral — A Genre Painting," *China Tourism*, Hong Kong: Hong Kong China Tourism Press, No. 104, Issue, pp. 38-39.

Huang, Soubao, *Ethnic Costume from Guizhou :Clothing Designs and Decorations from Minority Ethnic Groups in Southwest China*, Beijing: Foreign Languages Press, 1987. ASIN: 0835117383.

Hua, Nian, "Masks Expressing the Spirit of Nuo," *China Tourism,* Hong Kong: Hong Kong China Tourism Press, No. 104, pp. 4-9.

Hu, Chang-tu, "China, Its People, Its Society, Its Culture," *Survey of World Cultures*, Vol. 6, London: Mayflower, 1960.

Johnson, Charles, ed., *Myths, Legends and Folk Tales from the Hmong of Laos,* St. Paul: Macalaster College, 1985.

Jian, Sheng, "Complexities of Male Headgear," *China Tourism,* Vol. 104, Hong Kong: China Tourism Press, pp. 28-31.

Jiansu Fine Arts Publishing House, *Lao Fangz.: Dongzu Mulou, Old Houses: Timbered Structures of the Dong Minority Nationality,* Jiangsu. ISBN 7534405912.

Jun, Feng, "Days in Guizhou — Miao and Dong Stockades in the Province's Southeast," *China Tourism,* No. 104, Hong Kong: Hong Kong China Tourism Press, pp. 10-23.

Kanomi, Takako, *People of Myth: Textiles and Crafts of the Golden Triangle*.

Kendall, R. Eliott, *Beyond the Clouds: the Story of Samuel Pollard*, London: Cargate Press, 1954.

______________, *Eyes of the Earth: The Diary of Samuel Pollard*, London: Cargate Press, 1947.

Kuhn, D., *Science and Civilization in China, 5, IX, Textile Technology: Spinning and Reeling,* Cambridge: Cambridge University Press, 1988.

Kunstadter, Peter, ed., *Southeast Asian Tribes, Minorities and Nations*, Princeton: University Press, 1967.

Lan Lin, Phyllis and Christi Lan Lin, *Stories of Chinese Children's Hats, Symbolism and Folklore*, Indianapolis: University of Indianapolis Press, 1996. ISBN 1-880938-018.

Laumann, Maryta, ed., *Miao Textile Design*, Taipei: Fu Jen Catholic University Press, 1993.

Lee, Annette, translator, "Characteristics of Miao and Dong Cooking," *China Tourism*, No. 104, Hong Kong: China Tourism Hong Kong Press, p. 93.

Lewis, Paul and Elaine Lewis, *Peoples of the Golden Triangle, Six Tribes in Thailand*, London and New York: Thames and Hudson, 1984. ISBN 0-500-97314-8.

Li, Yuangui, *The Miao on Mount Leigong*, Guizhou National Press, 1988.

Lin, Ming Jin, ed., *Miao Tribe Adornment Art (Miao Zu Zhuang Ssi Yi Shu)*, Hunan Fine Arts Publishing. Unified Book Number: 8233.1126. Text in Mandarin.

Lin, Yeuh-Hwa (Lin Yaohua), "The Miao-Man Peoples of Kweichow," *Harvard Journal of Asiatic Studies 5,* 1940, pp. 261-344.

Lyman, Thomas Amis, *Dictionary of Mong Njua: A Miao (Meo) Language of Southeast Asia,* The Hague and Paris: Mouton & Co., 1974.

Ma, Yin, ed., *China's Minority Nationalities*, Beijing: Foreign Languages Press, 1989.

Mallinson, Jane, Nancy Donnelly and Ly Hang, *H'mong Batik: A Textile Technique from Laos,* Seattle: 1998.

McDaniel, Phila L., *Influence of Zen on Kannon in Japanese Art*, Long Beach: California State University at Long Beach, 1971.

______________, "The Collars of the Flower Miao of Nankai," *Ornament*, Fall 2001.

______________, "Tibetan Nomad Festivals," *Ornament*, Summer 2000.

______________, "Red Mahendranath Festival in Nepal," *Phi Delta Gamma Journal, 1970*.

Mickey, Margaret Portia, "The Cowrie Shell Miao of Kweichow," Cambridge: Peabody Museum, 1947.

Miller, Dorothy and Mary E. Cranston-Bennett, eds., *Indigo from Seed to Dye*, 8 vols., Aptos CA: Indigo Press, 1984. ISBN: 0960406018.

Miska, Maxine, *Folk Arts of Southeast Asia: Persistence and Change, Festival of American Folk Life*, Washington, D.C.: Smithsonian Institution and National Park Service, 1980.

Mottin, J., *The History of the Hmong (Meo, Miao)*, Bangkok: Rung Ruang Ratana Printing, 1980.

__________, *Fetes du Nouvel An Chez les Hmong Blanc de Thailande*, Bangkok: Don Bosco Press, 1980.

__________, *Contes et Legendes Hmong Blanc*, Bangkok: Don Bosco Press, 1980.

National Minority Literary and Art Team of the Central Institute for Nationalities and the Research Group of the Art Department of the Cultural Bureau, Kweichow Province, PRC, *Embroidery Designs of the Miao People of China*, Peking: The People's Fine Arts Publishing House, National Museum of History, 1956.

National Museum of History, *Chinese Embroidery*, Taipei: 1969.

National Museum of History, *Costumes and Accessories of Chinese Minorities, (Zhongguo Shaoshu Minzu Fushi)*, Taipei 2000.

National Tourism Administration, *Chinese Folk Festivals*, Beijing.

Needham, Joseph, *Science and Civilization in China*, Vol. 5, Part 9, (Ramie research), Cambridge: 1988, p. 16.

Nelson, Winnie, *The Guide to Asian Textile Collections*, Hong Kong: Textile Society of Hong Kong, 2000. ISBN 9628607715.

New Star Publishers, *Marriage Customs of Chinese Ethnic Minorities*, 1991. ISBN 7-80053-153-2.

Numrich, Charles H., *Living Tapestries*, Lima, Ohio: Fairway Press, 1945.

O'Connor, D., *Miao Costumes from Guizhou Province*, Farnham, England: James Hockey Gallery, West Surrey College of Art & Design,1994.

__________, "Best Bib and Tucker: Embroidery on Miao Jackets from Guizhou Province," *Embroidery*, Vol. 45, No. 3, Autumn 1994, pp. 152-4.

__________, "Using Hemp in Guizhou Province, Southwest China," *Journal for Weavers, Spinners and Dyers*, June 1994, pp. 26-8.

__________, "Textiles of the Miao Minority, Guizhou Province, Southwest China," *The Textile Society Magazine*, Vol. 21, Spring/Summer 1994, pp. 11-13.

Pollard, S., *The Sam Pollard Omnibus: Tight Corners on China — The Story of the Miao in Unknown China*, Pennsylvania: Woodburn Press, 1986.

Pourret, Jess G., *The Yao: The Mien and Mun Yao in China, Vietnam, Laos and Thailand*, Chicago: Art Media Resources, 2001. ISBN 1-58886-015-9.

Pu, Lu, *Designs of Chinese Indigo Batik*, New York: Lee Publishers Group/New World Press, 1981. ISBN: 0-86519-0143-3.

Qian, Yinyu, *Guizhou's Hidden Civilization*, PRC: June 1999. ISBN 7-102-02045-7/J.1754

Quincy, Keith, *Hmong: History of a People*, 1995.

Research Institute for the Study of Ethnic Groups in Southwest China, ed., *Studies of Ethnic Peoples in Southwest China*, Sichuan National Press, 1987.

Rossi, Gail, "A Flourishing Art – China: Guizhou Women Continure to Embroider Their Legends," *Threads*, Issue 9, February/March 1987, pp. 30-32.

__________, "Enduring Dress of the Miao, Guizhou Province, People's Republic of China," *Ornament*, Spring, 1988, pp. 29-31

__________, "Growing Indigo," *Surface Design Journal*, Oakland: Surface Design Association, 1988.

__________, "Miao Needlework," *Needlework & Thread*, May/June 1987, pp. 42-4.

__________, "Textiles from a Precious Place," (Exhibition announcement), *Threads*, Number 29, Newtown, CT: Taunton Press, June-July, 1990.

__________, *The Dong People of China — A Hidden Civilization*, Singapore: Hagley & Hoyle Pte Ltd., 1998.

__________, "Traditional Cross-stitch Among China's Remote Southwestern Provinces," *Counted Thread*, June 1986.

Ruey, Yih-fu, "The Miao, Their Origin and Southwestern Migration," Taipei: 1962.

Sandberg, Gosta, *Indigo Textiles: Technique and History*, Ashville, NC: Lark Books, 1986. ISBN: 0937274402.

Schein, Louisa, *Minority Rules, the Miao and the Feminine in China's Cultural Politics*, Duke University Press, 2000.

Schuster, Carl, "Relations of a Chinese Embroidery Design: Eastern Europe and Western Asia, Southeast Asia (The Dong Son Culture) and Melanesia," *Early Chinese Art and Its Possible Influence in the Pacific Basin*, New York: Asia Intercultural Arts Press, 1972.

Seiler-Baldinger, A., *Textiles: A Classification of Techniques*, Bathhurst, England: Crawford House Press, 1994.

Sen, Fu Xin and Hua Nian, *The Di Xi Masks in Anshun*, PRC: Hunan Fine Arts Publishing House, 1999. Text in Mandarin. ISBN 7-5356-1207-5 J.1127.

Shanghai Theatrical College, ed. com., *Ethnic Costumes and Clothing Decorations from China*, Chengdu: Hai Feng Publishing Comapany, Ltd., Sichuan People's Publishing House, 1986.

Sichuan National Press, Research Institute for the Study of Ethnic Groups in Southwest China, ed., *Studies of Ethnic Peoples in Southwest China*, Sichuan National Press, May, 1987.

Simonson, Throdis, *Flower Cloth of the Hmong*, Denver: Museum of Natural History, 1985

Sinclair, Kevin, *Forgotten Tribes of China*, Hong Kong: Intercontinental Publishing Corporation, Limited, 1987. LSN IBI. ISBN 0-920691-32-3.

Start, Laura E. and Mable C. Wright, "Decorated Textiles from Yunnan Collected by Augustine Henry, 1896-1898," *Memoirs of the Manchester Lit. and Phil. Society 80,* Manchester: The Victoria University of Manchester, 1935-36.

Sun, Zhenfa, Chief Editor and Zheng Zigang, Deputy Chief Editor, *Chinese Farmer Paintings*, Beijing: China Esperanto Press, 1996.

Szeto, Naomi Yin Yin and Valery M. Garre, *Children of the Gods, Dress and Symbolism in China,* Hong Kong: 1990. ISBN 962-7039-22-5.

Tian Cui, "Miao Embroidery: Reflections of Life and Legend," *China Tourism,* No. 104, pp. 24- 27.

Torimaru, Sadae, *Fabric Graffiti*, Tokyo. Text in Japanese. ISBN B167-0475-2.

Tracey, Lie-dan Lu, "From Barkcloth Beating to Silk Weaving: The Textile Industry from Pre-history to the Western Han Dynasty in South China," *The Textile Museum Journal*, Vol. 36 and 37, The Textile Museum, 1997-98. ISSN: 0083-7407.

Travel China Weekly, "Chabai Songfest of Bouyei Ethnic Group," *Travel China Weekly Newspaper*, 1999.

Wai Yin Club, "National Minority Costume of China Charity Show," *National Minority Costume of China*, Hong Kong: Hong Kong Joint Publishing Company, 1985. Text in Chinese.

Wan, Guodong, "Minority Lifestyles in Western Guizhou," *China Reconstructs*, Vol. XXXV, No. 8, August 1986, pp. 65-68.

Wang, Y., *Chinese Folk Embroidery*, Hong Kong: Commercial Press, 1987.

Wei, Ronghui, ed., *The Chinese National Culture of Costume and Adornment*, Beijing: China Textile Press.

Williams, C.A.S., *Outlines of Chinese Symbolism and Art Motives*, Peking: Customs College Press, 1921.

White, Virginia, *Pa ndau: The Needlework of the Hmong,* Cheney, WA: Cheney Free Press, 1982

Wong, How Man, "Peoples of China's Far Provinces," *National Geographic,* March, 1984, pp. 283-333.

Wu, Shishong and Introduction by Yu Qiuyu, *A Picture Album of China's Miao Costumes and Ornaments*, PRC: Guizhou People's Press, 2000. ISBN 7-221-05218-2/C74.

Xie, Shizun, "Encounters With the Yao in Their Mountain Home," *China Tourism,* No. 73, Hong Kong: Hong Kong Press, pp. 23-31.

Xinhua Publishing House, *Beautiful and Richly Endowed Southeast Guizhou*, Beijing: 1991. ISBN 7-5011-1368-8/F.132.

Xu, Lang et al., *Guiyang*, Beijing: New World Press, 1989.

Yang, Dequn et al., *Cultural Artifacts Used for Bodily Adornments Among the Ethnic Peoples of Yunnan*, Beijing: Wenwu Press, October 1991.

Yang, Sumin, "Fortune and Longevity Hats," *China Tourism,* No. 73, Hong Kong: China Tourism and Hong Kong Press, p. 72.

Yang Zhengwen, *The Miao Tribe's Costume and Culture*, Guiyang: Guizhou Nationalities Press. Text in Mandarin. ISBN 7- 54120784-5/Z.63.

Yang, Yang, ed., *An Appreciation and Analysis of the Costumes of Chinese Ethnic Minorities*, Taipei: Higher Education Press, August 1994.

Yixi, Xu, ed., *Headdresses of Chinese Minority Nationality Women*, PRC: China Film Press, China National Publishers, Importing and Exporting Corp., 1989.

Zeng, Xianyang, "The Guizhou Skirt Story," *China Tourism*, No. 104, Hong Kong: China Tourism Hong Kong Press.

Zhang, Boru, "Probing the Mystery of the Costume Arts of the Dong," *Echo Magazine*.

Zhao, Yu Chi and Kuang Shizhao, sr. eds. et al., *Clothings and Ornaments of China's Miao People,* Beijing: The Cultural Palace of Nationalities, 1985.

Zheng, Qi-ming, "An Introduction to Ancient Textiles," *Journal of Hong Kong Archaeological Society,* Vol. 13, 1992, p.118.

Zheng,Wen Yang, *Miao's Dress and Adornment*, PRC, 2000. Text in Mandarin. ISBN 5412-0784-5/Z.63.

Zhou, Xun and Gao Chunming, eds., *5000 Years of Chinese Costumes*, PRC: The Chinese Costumes Research Group of the Shanghai School of Traditional Operas, 1987.

International Advisory Board

RADM and MRS. W. HALEY ROGERS	Honorary Chairmen
AYDA AYOUB	Museum Liaison, Egypt
ELEANOR BEACH	American Art Historian
PROFESSOR KANEKO BISHOP	Tea Master, Omote-senke, School of Tea
PATRICIA C. DWINNELL BUTLER	Attorney, Retired Federal Judge
KATARINA REAL CATE	Anthropologist, South American Folk Art
JOYCE CORBETT	Textile Historian
MARIBEL G. DE COSIO	Museum Liaison, Mexico
ELIZABETH CUELLAR	Curator, International Folk Art Collection, University of Mexico
LESLIE GRACE	Folk Art and Textile Consultant
SOOK BOWER HANSEN	Museum Liaison, Korea
SAM and LESLIE HINTON	Folklorists
JOYCE HUNDAL	India Consultant
EDWARD INSKEEP	Planning Consultant, United Nations
GOTTFRIED KUMPF	Painter, Museum Liaison, Austria
MARK JOHNSON	Indonesia Consultant
JACK LENOR LARSEN	Textile Designer and Author
M. C. MADHAVAN, Ph.D.	Professor, SDSU, International Development
HRH PRINCESS MARINA	Museum Liaison, Greece
STEFAN MAX, Ph.D.	European Linguist and Cultural Liaison
THE HONORABLE MARILYN L. MENNELLO	
and MICHAEL A. MENNELLO	Founders, The Mennello Museum of American Folk Art
JOHN DARCY NOBLE	Curator Emeritus, Museum of the City of New York
JOHN NORTON	Honorary Consul of Sweden
NIKI de SAINT PHALLE	Renowned Sculptor, Museum Liaison, France
GENE SAPPER	Consul of Guatemala
HAKU SHAH	Authority on Tribal and Folk Art of India
TATSUZO SHIMAOKA	Potter and a Living National Treasure of Japan
OPPI UNTRACHT	Artist / Craftsman - Jeweler, Author, Museum Liaison, Finland
ELIZABETH VANDER	Museum Liaison, The Philippines
VIRA WILLIAMS	President, Tema, Ghana, West Africa / San Diego Sister City Society
SORI YANAGI	Industrial Designer, Director, Mingeikan, Tokyo

Museum Connoisseurs *Dedicated to building the Museum's collection*

CHARMAINE and MAURICE KAPLAN, CHAIRMEN

APRIL and LOWELL BLANKFORT
PATRICIA C. DWINNELL BUTLER
LEE and ALLEN CHAO
MARY and DALLAS CLARK
DAVID C. COPLEY
HELEN K. COPLEY
SUE K. and CHARLES G. EDWARDS
AUDREY GEISEL
JOHN HARDY and JEAN HAHN HARDY
JOAN and IRWIN JACOBS
JAMES P. and JUDITH A. KEMP
HELEN W. KORMAN
ARMAND J. LABBÉ
BARBARA JOY MARRICTT-WILCOX
CHRISTA McREYNOLDS
BETTY-JO PETERSEN
NIKI de SAINT PHALLE
JIM and NORMA SLONE
MINA and ED SMITH
MARY ANN and BOB STUBBS
RON and MARY TAYLOR
JOHN and CHRISTY WALTON
JOANNE C. and FRANK R. WARREN
VALERIE B. and MARTIN H. WEBSTER
FRANCES HAMILTON WHITE
CAROLYN YORSTON

Corporate Sponsors

Bank of America Private Bank
BIOCOM
Eller Media Company
J. R. Filanc Construction Company
The McGraw-Hill Companies
Resource Associates
Ridout Plastics
San Diego Sports Arena
Union Bank of California

Corporate Associates

Bob Baker Foundation
Karl Strauss Breweries
Nordstrom
PaineWebber
Rancho Self Storage
The Thursday Club

Publication

Design and Editing | MARTHA W. LONGENECKER

ROB SIDNER

Photography | PHILA McDANIEL — the land and the people

LYNTON GARDINER — studio photography of art objects

Production Assistance | ANN S. BETHEL, Ph.D.

ADRIANNE O. BRATIS

TERRI BRYSON

JAKE HARSHBARGER

JEREMIAH MALONEY

ANTHONY SCOGGINS

GRETCHEN VAN CAMP

Typesetting | WESTERFIELD TYPESETTING & GRAPHICS

Printing | TOPPAN PRINTING CO., TOKYO

Mingei International is a non-profit, public foundation supported
by memberships and contributions. The museum program is funded
in part by the City of San Diego Commission for Arts and Culture
and the County of San Diego Community Enhancement Program